EVANGELISTIC TRAINING AND CHRISTIAN APOLOGETICS

Gary L. Beaty

Evangelistic Training and Christian Apologetics
Copyright © 2022 Gary L. Beaty. All rights reserved.
ISBN 979-8-218-10504-4

Published by:
Gary L. Beaty
300 S.E. 35th Street
Keystone Heights, Fl. 32656

Manufactured in the United States of America

Acknowledgements

---・◆・---

First and foremost, I would like to recognize my loving wife, Diane. Outside of the Lord, she was and is my greatest inspiration, for whom I am forever thankful. Her sincerity before the Lord challenged me in such a way that helped me find Jesus as my personal Lord and Savior.

I would like to acknowledge Pastor Doug and his wife, Mary Ellen Willett. Pastor Doug comforted Diane and I when we were a young married couple at our stillborn son's graveside service. We soon thereafter started attending Haverhill Baptist Church where Doug was the Pastor. I understand that Pastor Doug has recently gone on to be with the Lord. He and Mary Ellen were truly used of the Lord to guide and inspire our lives.

I would like to acknowledge Terry Sams who was instrumental in our lives, who invited us to attend Haverhill Baptist Church where she was the leader of a young married couple's class.

I would like to acknowledge Steve and Sally Kern. Steve and Sally also attended our young married couple's class. Steve was studying to be a pastor at Palm Beach Atlantic College at that time. They both were very instrumental in helping me to understand what it means to put your whole faith in Christ alone as your Savior.

I would like to acknowledge Bill and Marge Moyer who also attended our young married couple's class. Bill was also studying to be a pastor at Palm Beach Atlantic College at that time. Marge then took over the role as the leader of the young married couple's class. Diane and I both really enjoyed being a part of this class with its Bible study and times of fellowship. We both look back with fond memories at the times we had in conversational prayer in their home. For which I was very thankful, Marge gave me her Thompson Chain Reference Bible at that time. With Steve Kern's encouragement, I took over the leadership role of the young married couple's class when Bill and Marge left to go to seminary to further his education.

I would also like to acknowledge Pastor Brandon Denmark, Pastor of Trinity Baptist Church, who was kind enough to help me edit this book.

I would also like to acknowledge and thank my son, David Aaron Beaty, for helping me to process the book and for sharing with me his knowledge of the world of books.

Foreword

"Having read many books on evangelism and apologetics, I can say that very few do as good a job at teaching a simple, yet thorough Biblical understanding of these subjects as does *Evangelistic Training and Christian Apologetics*. This book would make a great resource for a small group study, a Sunday School class, or even a new believer's class. It does not encourage a "canned" gospel presentation as so many do but helps the believer to be grounded in the basic truths of God's Word so that he or she can share openly and honestly about Jesus from their own personal knowledge of Him and His Word. I encourage any believer who wants to sharpen their evangelistic skills and grow deeper in their knowledge of God's Word to read this book."

Pastor Brandon Denmark
Senior Pastor
Trinity Baptist Church

TABLE OF CONTENTS

Chapter 1
Personal Preparation

Having Your Own Assurance of Salvation .... Page 1
Be Filled with the Spirit
(Ephesians 5:17-18, Galatians 5:22-25) .... Page 1
Parable of the Sower Matthew 13:3-4, 18-19........... Page 5
The Gospel (Our Role and God's Role) .... Page 7
The Gospel (A Team Effort)................................. Page 8
Common Ground and Our Testimony .... Page 9
A Gentle Tongue Can Break a Bone
(Proverbs 25:15) .... Page 12
Distractions (Seed Sown Among Thorns)
Matthew 13: 7,22 .... Page 14
Distractions (The Busyness of Life)
II Timothy 2:3-4 .... Page 15
The Fear of Man is a Snare (Proverbs 29:25) .... Page 16
Do We Walk the Talk? or Are We a Noisy Gong?... Page 19
Speak the Word with Authority .... Page 20

Chapter 2
The Message

Who is Jesus?
(For Those Who May Not Really Know) .... Page 23
Jesus is the Only Way to God .... Page 24
The Baptism of Jesus .... Page 26
The Temptation of Christ Matthew 4:1-5 .... Page 28
The Bronze Snake .... Page 30
The Gospel of Peace Ephesians 6:15 .... Page 33
The Workers in the Vineyard .... Page 41

Chapter 3
Biblical Answers to Objections

I'm a Pretty Good Person .... Page 45
I Don't Want to Leave My Friends .... Page 49
I Don't Need a Savior .... Page 51
For Those Who Say, Not Now .... Page 53

Chapter 4
Christian Apologetics

Science and the Bible .... Page 57
Prophecy Fulfilled .... Page 60

Annotated Bibliography .... Page 62

Fair Use Policy

This document may contain copyrighted material, the use of which has not been specifically authorized by the copyright owner.

I, Gary L. Beaty, am making this book available in my effort to advance the understanding of the gospel of Jesus Christ. I believe that this constitutes a "fair use" of the copyrighted material as provided for in section 107 of the US Copyright Law.

If you wish to use this copyrighted material for purposes of your own that go beyond "fair use," you must obtain permission from the copyright owner.

If your copyrighted material appears in this book and you disagree with my assessment that it constitutes "fair use," please contact me.

INTRODUCTION

The content of this book is intended to be used to help equip the Christian to be able to have an evangelistic conversation with an unbeliever. The format of this book is primarily designed to provide the Christian with scripture and commentary that is geared toward lifestyle evangelism.

Due to the large amount of scripture contained herein, it is not reasonable to think that one should memorize all these referenced scriptures. The intent of this book rather, is to help the Christian become more familiar with these Bible passages as they relate to evangelism. As we need to share a specific scripture with someone, we could rather show that person the scripture from a highlighted pocket New Testament. We should, of course, have enough scripture memorized that we can readily share the gospel at any given time.

BIBLE REFERENCES

Scripture quotations taken from The Holy Bible, New International Version ® NIV ® Copyright © 1973, 1978, 1984, 2011, by Biblica, Inc. TM All rights reserved worldwide, excepting those Scriptures noted and quoted from the King James Version and except those Scriptures quoted in the section entitled, **Chapter 1, Personal Preparation,** "Be Filled with the Spirit", which is Scripture taken from the NEW AMERICAN STANDARD BIBLE, ©1960, 1962, 1963, 1968, 1971, 1973, 1975, 1977, by The Lockman Foundation and those NASB Scriptures noted and quoted elsewhere.

The Scripture quotations noted above do not exceed the limits imposed by the NIV or the NASB whereby written permission must be obtained from them.

CHAPTER 1

PERSONAL PREPARATION

Having Your Own Assurance of Salvation

First, we must be sure of our own salvation. (Romans 8:15, Galatians 4:1-6) When we believe on Christ to be our Lord and Savior, God sends his Holy Spirit to take control of our lives. He comes into our very being at which time His Spirit bears witness with our spirit that we are a child of God. God, by His Spirit assures us that we have been born again by His Spirit from above.

Be Filled with the Spirit
(Ephesians 5:17-18, Galatians 5:22-25)

This passage in Ephesians is literally translated *"Be being filled with the Spirit"*, indicating an ongoing need to be filled with God's Spirit. Galatians 5:16 tells us to *"… walk by the Spirit."* In Colossians 2:6-7 the apostle Paul had this to say about walking in the Spirit. *(6) "As you therefore have received Christ Jesus the Lord, so walk in Him, (7) having been firmly rooted and now being built up in Him and established in your faith, just as you were instructed, and overflowing with gratitude."* From this passage we see that our walk in the Spirit as believers is to be conducted in the same way we initially received Christ Jesus as our Lord and Savior. So, the question is, <u>what was involved and how did we receive</u> Christ?

(1)<u>We heard God's Word.</u> Romans 10:17 tells us that the Word imparts faith. *"So, faith comes from hearing and hearing by the word of Christ."* John 6:63 tells us that the Word imparts life. *"It is the Spirit who gives life; the flesh profits nothing; the words that I have spoken to you are spirit and are life."* Luke 4:4 tells us that the Word is essential to live. *"And Jesus answered him 'It is written, Man Shall Not Live on Bread Alone".* This is a quote from Deuteronomy 8:3, which has an additional statement: *"...but man lives by everything that proceeds out of the mouth of the Lord."* Psalms 1:1-2 tells us to meditate on God's Word. *(1) "How blessed is the man who does not walk in the counsel of the wicked, Nor stand in the path of sinners, Nor sit in the seat of scoffers! (2) But his delight is in the law of the Lord, And in His law, he meditates day and night."* Colossians 3:16 tells us to memorize God's Word. *"Let the Word of Christ richly dwell within you..."* James 1:22 tells us to do what the Word says. *"But prove yourselves doers of the Word, and not merely hearers who delude themselves."* Revelation 1:3 tells us to read the Word, which says,

"Blessed is he who reads and those who hear the words of the prophecy and heed the things which are written in it; for the time is near." Second Timothy 2:15 tells us to study the Word. *"Study to shew thyself approved unto God, a workman that needeth not to be ashamed, rightly dividing the word of truth."* (KJV)

(2) <u>We saw our need for Christ to be our Lord and Savior</u>. As it relates to our initial salvation, in Matthew 5:3, Jesus taught us in the sermon on the mount that the first beatitude is, *"Blessed are the poor in spirit, for theirs is the kingdom of heaven."* In the parable of the Pharisee and the tax collector, recorded in Luke 18:9-14, it was the tax collector who asserted that he had no righteousness of his own but rather in verse 13 said, *"God, be merciful to me, the sinner!"* Before we can have a savior, we must realize that we truly are a sinner. As the old hymn Rock of Ages says, "Nothing in my hand do I bring, but only to the cross do I cling." As it relates to our Christian walk after our conversion, the apostle Paul declares in Romans 7:18, *"For I know that nothing good dwells in me, that is, in my flesh."* The sinful nature is sometimes translated *"the flesh."* This is the old adamic fallen self-centered nature we inherited from Adam. Paul wrote this passage in Romans 7 as a believer who still had to deal with his old sinful nature. Jesus told his disciples in John 15:5, *"I am the vine; you are the branches; he who abides in Me, and I in him, he bears much fruit; for apart from me you can do nothing."*

(3) <u>In and through our salvation in Christ, God has given us everything we need to lead a full and fruitful life for Him</u>. Second Peter 1:3 tells us that, *"seeing that His divine power has granted to us everything pertaining to life and godliness, through the true knowledge of Him who called us by His own glory and excellence."* (See also Colossians 2:9-10, Ephesians 1:3, Philippians 4:13.)

(4) <u>We appropriate this fullness by faith by living the co-crucified/co-risen life of Christ.</u> (Galatians 2:20) The apostle Paul expounds on this in Romans 6:8-13. In verse 11 it says, *"In the same way, **count** yourselves dead to sin but alive to God in Christ Jesus."* (NIV) In the King James Version this verse tells us to *"Likewise **reckon** ye also yourselves to be dead indeed unto sin, but alive unto God through Jesus Christ our Lord."* These words *"reckon",* in the King James and *"count"* in the New International Version are accounting terms. They carry the idea of looking at the ledger of our lives from God's perspective as we have trusted in Christ to be our Lord and Savior. According to God's record, God has already executed the sentence of death upon our sinful selves in Christ and has given us the righteousness of Christ by His resurrection. This righteousness is an imputed righteousness bestowed on all those who believe in Him. This is our perfect position in Christ in which we are secure in Him. Out of love and a thankful heart, we are admonished to, by an act of our will, bring the condition of our daily lives into conformity

with this position. We do this by yielding to God's will and by saying no to sin. We should do this by concentrating on being *"alive unto God"* through the power of the resurrection of Christ working in us. In this way, the sinful ways of our *"old self"* will be more incidental. We do not need to become introspective about ourselves in our shortcomings and failures, but rather we are to get on with our lives by confessing and forsaking our sin according to I John 1:5-9. (See also Romans 12:2) In Colossians 3:1-14, the apostle Paul describes this walk of faith as the putting off our old sinful self as if it were a dirty garment and the putting on of a new garment of *(10) "… the new self, who is being renewed to a true knowledge according to the image of the One who created him."* Here he lists certain sins and sinful attitudes that he admonishes us to put off and certain fruit of the Spirit that we are to put on. This list is not exhaustive. (See also Romans 13:14) We know that the fruit of the spirit is from the Holy Spirit as we yield to Him. (Ephesians 5:18 and Galatians 5:22-23)

Parable of the Sower
Matthew 13:3-4, 18-19
(Seed Sown Along the Path)
(The Resistant Hearer)

As we share the gospel, we need to be sensitive to the spiritual need and condition of the person we are sharing with. This would also include perceiving how receptive the person is to the gospel.

In these verses Jesus is talking about a person who is resistant and nonreceptive. The person is compared to a hard packed path in which the seed does not penetrate the soil. Luke 8:5 expounds on this stating that the seed and path are *"trampled on"*, indicating that the hearer has allowed the ways of man to dissuade him from the truth of God's Word. In Matthew 13:19 it is said that the *hearer "does not understand it"* (the Word). This term *"understand"* is not talking about an intellectual understanding of the Word, but rather, a willful rejection of the impact that it would have on their lives. To get a better sense of this, see also Psalms 32:9, Proverbs 18:2, Isaiah 27:11, Isaiah 44:19, and Jeremiah 4:22. Jesus said in John 7:17 *"If anyone chooses to do God's will, he will find out whether my teaching comes from God or whether I speak on my own."* Even though the intellect is used in part of our acceptance of Christ into our lives, it is only a part. For example, as it relates to the intellect, Jesus invited Thomas to examine the nail prints in His hands and the scar where the spear was thrusted into His side as evidence of His death and resurrection. The main problem is man's sinful will, (John 3:19). We cannot win a person over to Christ just by trying to prove who Christ is intellectually. That person needs to come to a place in their life where they are willing to let Christ take over the control of their lives. As those who share the gospel, we need to recognize that the problem with the person characterized as being a hard packed trodden path is a willful problem and not an intellectual one. Consequently, we should not expect that our repeated arguments for the acceptance of Biblical teaching on an intellectual level will persuade that person to accept Christ. In fact, it may cause that person to be even more resistant to it. Instead, we may need to just live out our Christian lives before them as we pray for their salvation. Quite often this is the situation we face with some of our lost family members and loved ones. Due to the hardheartedness of this person, the seed of God's word will not penetrate the soil. Therefore, sometimes God has to breakup that resistance by utilizing certain situations, circumstances, and the negative consequences of that person's life to bring them to a point of being more receptive to God's Word (the gospel). We see this in the parable of the lost son in Luke 15:11-14 and the historical account of the life of Nebuchadnezzar recorded in Daniel 4:19-37.

The Gospel
(Our Role and God's Role)

As we discern the receptivity level of the person we are sharing with, this should help us to share with that person more effectively. To throw more light on this, the apostle Paul wrote the following in I Corinthians

3:5-8, *(5) "What after all is Apollos? And what is Paul? Only servants, through whom you came to believe-as the Lord has assigned to each his task. (6) I planted the seed, Apollos watered it, but God has been making it grow. (7) So, neither the one who plants nor the one who waters is anything, but only God, who makes things grow. (8) The one who plants and the one who waters have one purpose, and they will each be rewarded according to their own labor."* Jesus spoke to this issue in the Parable of the Growing Seed written in Mark 4:26-29. The point of this is that we, as God's laborers planting the seed, do not fully comprehend how God's Word produces God's desired effect. God is the one who does this. We are told in John 6:44 that, *"No one comes to Me unless the Father who sent Me draws him, and I will raise him up at the last day."* We see from this verse that it is God the Father who draws people to Jesus. Having said this, Jesus also said in John 12:32, *"But I, when I am lifted up from the earth, I will draw all men to Myself."* Our role is to lift up Christ (share the gospel). God's role is to miraculously draw that person into a saving faith relationship with Himself.

The Gospel
(A Team Effort)

Another passage that illustrates workers working in the field with evangelism is found in John 4:34-38, which says, *(34) "My food, said Jesus, 'is to do the will of Him who sent me and to finish His work. (35) Don't you have a saying, 'It's still four months until harvest'? I tell you, open your eyes and look at the fields! They are ripe for harvest. (36) Even now the one who reaps draws a wage and harvests a crop for eternal life, so that the sower and the reaper may be glad together. (37) Thus, the saying 'One sows, and another reaps' is true. (38) I sent you to reap what you have not worked for. Others have done the hard work, and you have reaped the benefits of their labor."* Connecting this idea of God's workers either planting, working the soil, watering, and reaping a harvest, with recognizing the receptivity level of the hearers that we read about in the parable of the sower, this should help guide us as we share the gospel with a particular person. As we discern this receptivity level, we should plant, cultivate, water, or perhaps even to reap them into God's kingdom. We should do this remembering what we read before that it is *"only God who makes things grow."* It also might be that over the course of time, God will use several people as instruments to help a person come to a saving faith relationship with Christ.

Common Ground and Our Testimony

As we communicate with and learn more about the kind of person, we are trying to share Christ with, we can identify points of common experience with that person. Our objective is to try to show that person that the most common thing we all share is that we are all sinners in need of a savior. The apostle Paul speaks to this issue in I Corinthians 9:19-23. In verse 22 he summarizes this by saying, *"I have become all things to all men so that by all possible means I might be able to save some."* In this passage Paul shows that he is identifying with the group or person he is addressing from a common background. In doing so, I believe that he hopes that they in turn will identify with him. As they see the truth of the impact of how the gospel has transformed his life, this lends credibility to the gospel message. We as believers, are God's letter to a lost world (II Corinthians 3:2-3).

In his letter to the Ephesians in Chapter 6:13-17, the apostle Paul admonishes the church to put on the full armor of God. From an evangelistic standpoint, notice how Ephesians 6:15 tells us that we are to have our *"… feet fitted with the readiness that comes from the gospel of peace."* In the NASB it says, *"and having shod your feet with the preparation of the gospel of peace;"* Certainly, in part, he is referring to our being ready and able to share the gospel. (See also II Timothy 2:15 and II Timothy 4:2.) It may be in some instances that we may also want to share our personal testimony as a means of identifying with that person. As we reflect on and prepare to share our personal testimony, sometimes it is helpful if we share with that person from our common experience. As much as honestly possible, share those areas of your life that are common with the person's life to whom you are speaking. We have many aspects to our testimony from which we can do this. We need to think in broad terms as we do this. For example, our life before Christ might have been like that of the prodigal son, or we may have been more like his brother in that story, self- righteous but religious. Or, we may have been like Saul of Tarsus before he became the apostle Paul, an antagonist toward anything Christian. Maybe we identify most with being a Gentile (an unchurched person). Or, maybe we thought of ourselves as being a good religious person, without any inner peace that comes from the assurance of salvation, etc. We, of course need to share how our lives have been transformed after receiving Christ as our Lord and Savior.

Of course, it is not necessary that we use our personal testimony as we already said that our most common ground is that we are all lost sinners in need of a perfect savior. (Ephesians 2:1-3)

Irrespective of whether we use our personal testimony or not, we must make sure that our message stays focused on the gospel. The apostle Paul put it this way in I Corinthians 2:2, *"For I resolved to know nothing while I was with you except Jesus Christ and Him crucified."* (The gospel according to the apostle Paul is summarized in his letter to the Corinthians in I Corinthians 15:1-4.)

A Gentle Tongue Can Break a Bone
(Proverbs 25:15)

In Jude:3, we are told to contend for the faith. But the question is, how do we contend for the faith in an increasingly contentious world. The apostle Paul gives us some guidance on this in his letter to Timothy in II Timothy 2:22-26. In this passage Paul is instructing Timothy to avoid stupid arguments because they produce quarrels. He then says in verse 24, *"And the Lord's servant must not be quarrelsome but must be kind to everyone, able to teach, not resentful."* In verse 25 he says, *"Opponents must be gently instructed..."*. Here we see that the apostle instructs Timothy and us to be kind and gentle toward everyone just as he does also in his letter to Titus in Chapter 3:2. He then goes on to say in II Timothy 2:25,26 that as we do this, we do so *(25)"...in the hope that God will grant them repentance leading them to a knowledge of the truth, (26) and that they will come to their senses and escape the trap of the devil, who has taken them captive to do his will."* From this we see that people will be more likely to respond to the gospel if we deliver it in a spirit of gentleness and love. (Ephesians 4:15)

We see from these two passages that there are three things mentioned that will enable us to do this in love. The first one is that we see the person that we are sharing with from God's perspective and that is that they are being held captive by the devil. We see from this that God has enlisted us to be a part of His rescue team. As part of that team, with the message of the gospel, He will use us to liberate those being held captive by the devil. From verse 26 we also see that the person's will is involved in whether they either want to be rescued or see their need to be rescued. The devil, as the tempter, uses the deceitfulness of sin (Hebrews 3:12-13) to entrap the person. He tempts man to either try to establish his own salvation through religious practices or to believe that he does not need to be saved. In this situation he tempts man to either believe that God does not exist or that God simply overlooks our sin and that there is no punishment for our sin. The truth of the gospel message, when properly presented, exposes the damming lies of these sinful lifestyles. According to Titus 3:3, the second thing that will help us to speak to that person in love is to remember that we too were opponents of God, who were in the same lost condition as those to whom we are sharing. The third thing that will enable us to share with that person in love according to Titus 3:4-7, is to look to Jesus as our supreme example in the way He has dealt with us in His lovingkindness toward us all. Proverbs 15:1 tells us, *"A gentle answer turns away wrath, but a harsh word stirs up anger."*

But then the apostle Paul goes on to tell Timothy in II Timothy 3:1-5, that he will encounter people who are so steeped in all kinds of sins that he would do well to separate himself from these people. No amount of intellectual appeal to them will overcome their stubborn sinful will in the love of their sin. This goes back to the issue that we addressed in the section recognizing the spiritual level of the person that we are sharing with. We covered this in our commentary about the seed that fell on the wayside in the parable of the sower.

Distractions
(Seed Sown Among Thorns)
Matthew 13: 7,22

It is debatable whether this passage is referring to unbelievers or believers. I believe that it is possible for us as believers to also become distracted with the issues of worry, with the cares of this life and the lust for wealth and other things to the point that we lead unfruitful lives. We need to guard ourselves against these issues. We can do this by reminding ourselves and obeying what Jesus taught in the sermon on the mount recorded in Matthew 6:19-21, and 24, which says, *(19) "Do not store up for yourselves treasures on earth, where moths and vermin destroy, and where thieves break in and steal. (20) But store up for yourselves treasures in heaven where moths and vermin do not destroy, and where thieves do not break in and steal. (21) For where your treasure is, there your heart will be also. (24) No one can serve two masters. Either you will hate the one and love the other, or you will be devoted to the one and despise the other. You cannot serve both God and money."*

As it relates to the issue of worrying about having the necessities of this life, Jesus addressed this also in His sermon on the mount in Matthew's Gospel in Chapter 6:25-34. Jesus assures us that God will supply our needs. Jesus concluded this part of His sermon in verses 33 and 34, by saying, *(33) "But seek first His kingdom and His righteousness and all these things will be given to you as well. (34) Therefore, do not worry about tomorrow, for tomorrow will worry about itself. Each day has enough trouble of its own."* The apostle Paul writes in his letter to the Philippians in Philippians 4:6,7 the following, *(6) "Do not be anxious about anything, but in every situation, by prayer and petition, with thanksgiving, present your request to God. (7) And the peace of God, which transcends all understanding, will guard your hearts and minds in Christ Jesus."*

Distractions
(The Busyness of Life)
II Timothy 2:3-4

In this passage, the apostle Paul tells Timothy and us to *(3) "Join with me in suffering, like a good soldier of Christ Jesus. (4) No one serving as a soldier gets entangled in civilian affairs, but rather tries to please his commanding officer."* I take this to mean that we should not allow the busyness of this life to distract us from our primary mission in life. This means that we see ourselves as ambassadors for Christ first and foremost even as we go about the everyday affairs of this life.

In Colossians 4:3 the apostle Paul instructs Timothy and us to *"... pray for us too, that God may open a door for our message, so that we may proclaim the mystery of Christ for which I am in chains."* When God *"opens a door"* for us to share, we could look at it as a divine appointment or opportunity that God has placed before us even in the everyday routine of our lives. We will be more apt to recognize these opportunities if we are praying for them and leading our lives as a soldier for Christ and not as a civilian.

The Fear of Man is a Snare
(Proverbs 29:25)

Why is it sometimes we shy away from sharing the gospel when we know we should? As it relates to sharing the Christian message, the apostle Paul had this to say to Timothy and us in II Timothy 1:6-8, which says, *(6) "For this reason I remind you to fan into flame the gift of God, which is in you through the laying on of my hands. (7) For the Spirit God gave us does not make us timid, but gives us power, love and self-discipline, (8) So do not be ashamed of the testimony about our Lord or of me His prisoner. Rather, join with me in suffering for the gospel, by the power of God."* In the King James Version verse *(7)* says, *"For God hath not given us a spirit of fear; but of power and of love, and of a sound mind."* As we look at this overall passage, the apostle Paul admonishes Timothy and us not to be ashamed of the gospel and the persecution connected with it. (See verses 5, 12, and 16.) The context here is one of not being afraid of real persecution and or being ashamed of the stigma (from the world's viewpoint) of imprisonment and punishment. Given the religious freedoms that we have enjoyed as a free society, we as Americans know very little of what it means to be really persecuted. At the time of writing this paper however, this may not be the case soon.

As it relates to sharing the gospel, the question is, what are we afraid of?

We have the fear of man when:

we may be afraid of offending someone causing them to become angry with us.

we may be afraid that the person we are sharing with may become confrontational.

we may even be afraid of being humiliated by someone who takes a position of superiority, who may denigrate us.

we may be just afraid of what that person thinks about us.

in an ongoing relationship with someone such as a family member, or friend or co- worker etc., we may be afraid of being shunned.

At the core of this fear of man is our pride in which we are more concerned about what other people might think about us than we are in pleasing God through sharing His message. As a negative example of this kind of fear of man, we find it in the person of the apostle Peter when the apostle Paul reproved him for being a hypocrite. In that situation, Peter withdrew from the Gentile believers refusing to eat with them for fear of what the men sent from James might think of him. (James was the leader of the Jerusalem church.) (Galatians 2:11-14)

How do we overcome this fear? We do it by reflecting on how much God loves us. First John 4:18,19 tells us that, *(18) "There is no fear in love, but perfect love drives out fear… (19) "We love because He first loved us."* When our love relationship with Christ is right, we then seek to please God rather than being more concerned about what others may think about us or act toward us. We do this by being obedient to God, which includes sharing the gospel, sometimes despite our feelings.

As a beautiful example of this kind of love for Jesus, we find it recorded in Mark 14:3-9. In this account, Mary anoints Jesus's head with a very expensive perfume. Some of the people there were indignant at this, rebuking her harshly. Being a woman, in a society dominated by men, Mary dared to show her love for Jesus at the risk of this kind of reproof and rejection. Jesus then defended her, telling those who were criticizing her, that she was to be commended for this act of love. As for showing this kind of courage and love, Jesus then held her up as an example to all of us in verse *(9)* which says, *"Truly I tell you, wherever the gospel is preached throughout the world, what she has done will also be told in memory of her."*

In conclusion, we read the following from Hebrews 13:12-13, *(12), "And so Jesus also suffered outside the city gate to make the people holy through His own blood. (13) Let us, then, go to Him outside the camp, bearing the disgrace he bore."* The place being referred to as being outside the city gate or outside the camp is a place of rejection. The question is, are we willing to go outside the camp in our love for Jesus despite what others may think of us?

Do We Walk the Talk?
or
Are We a Noisy Gong?

I Thessalonians 4:11,12 tells us, *(11) "and make it your ambition to lead a quiet life: You should mind your own business and work with your hands, just as we told you, (12) so that your daily life may win the respect of outsiders and so that you will not need to be dependent on anybody."* Colossians 4:5 tells us to *"Be wise in the way you act toward outsiders; make the most of every opportunity."* (See also I Peter 2:12) In these scriptures, the apostle Paul and the apostle Peter are telling us that we are, through our speech and conduct, to win the respect of outsiders in and through our daily lives. The question is, does our conduct before and with them match our Christian profession? If not, we have become a reproach to them. The apostle Paul put it this way in I Corinthians 13:1, *"If I speak in the tongues of men or of angels, but do not have love, I am only a resounding gong or a clanging cymbal."* The sound of a noisy resounding gong or a clanging cymbal is an irritant that no one wants to listen to. This is what our Christian profession sounds like when our daily conduct contradicts it.

This does not mean, of course, that we live sinless lives. (I John 1:8) It may mean however that we may have to ask someone to forgive us, or that we may need to make amends or restitution with someone. Or it may be that we need to admit to our not being a good example before them. We, of course, need to do this with a repentant attitude.

To summarize, Jesus tells us in the sermon on the mount in Matthew 5:16, *"… let your light shine before others, that they may see your good deeds and glorify your Father in heaven."*

Speak the Word with Authority

In his letter to *"God's elect"* scattered abroad, the apostle Peter had this to say in I Peter 4:11, *"If anyone speaks, they should do so as one who speaks the very words of God."* The apostle Paul put it this way in II Corinthians 2:17, *"… in*

Christ, we speak before God with sincerity, as those sent from God." According to these scriptures we are to speak the Word of God authoritatively. This means that we do not believe that truth is subjective, but rather that the God of the Bible is the sole source of truth. Romans 3:4 tells us *"… Let God be true, and every human being a liar."* It is from this position that we speak.

Given the opportunity, we could also share that this truth is personified in the person of the Lord Jesus Christ. Jesus boldly made this claim of Himself in John's Gospel in chapter 14, verse 6, which says, *"Jesus answered, I am the way, and the truth and the life. No one comes to the Father except through Me."* Throughout the Gospels Jesus boldly asserted and demonstrated that He was the Son of God. (Luke 22:69-70, John 10:30-33, 37-38, John 12:45, John 14:7-10)

There are only three possibilities as to who Christ was, given the fact He claimed to be God. Those were:

He was a charlatan.

He was deluded.

He is God. **(1)**

This does not leave room for Him being just another moral teacher.

CHAPTER 2

THE MESSAGE

Who is Jesus?
(For Those Who May Not Really Know)

Jesus is God the Father's only begotten Son. He is the second person of the triune God. He is fully God, but He is also fully man. He existed in eternity past with the Father and the Holy Spirit as the one triune God. He was born of a virgin woman, conceived by God the Holy Spirit. Hence it was told of Him to also call His name Immanuel, which means God is with us. (John 1:1-2, 14, Matthew 1:22-23) Through the power of God the Holy Spirit, He performed countless miracles for three years as part of His teaching and preaching ministry. Being He had no earthly father, He had no sinful nature, therefore, in obedience to God the Father, He led a sinless life. Thus, only He was qualified to be the perfect sacrifice to God for our sin as the perfect Lamb of God. (John 1:29, John 3:16) He did this by allowing Himself to be crucified at the hands of the Jewish leaders and the Romans. He rose from the dead and ascended into heaven where He is seated at the right hand of God the Father. (Acts 1:3,9, Hebrews 10:12, 12:2) Seated at God's right hand, He is presently interceding for us and our salvation. (Hebrews 7:25)

Jesus is the Only Way to God

Matthew 7:13-14	The Narrow Gate
John 14:6	The Way the Truth and the Life
I Timothy 2:5	One Mediator
Acts 4:12	No Salvation in Any Other Name Other Than Jesus

Our society is becoming increasingly resistant to the idea that Jesus is the only way to God. The idea that there are several ways in which a person can express their life's view about God and spiritual beliefs is somewhat expressed in a pervasive attitude which says, "Everyone has the right to his or her own opinion." This attitude however, flies in the face of the fact that there is truth and that anything outside of that truth is error. The apostle Paul tells us in Romans 3:4 to *"...Let God be true and every human being a liar..."* Jesus boldly proclaimed in John 14:6 that *"I am the way and the truth and the life. No one comes to the Father except through me."*

In their non-acceptance of this truth, this person's attitude, in the name of tolerance, fails to:

(1) recognize the absolute holiness of God. (Exodus 15:11, Revelation 15:4) Therefore, He is unapproachable except through the way He has provided in Christ (I Timothy 6:15-18)

(2) recognize that God commands us to be holy. (Hebrews 12:14, I Peter 1:16, II Peter 3:11) Religion in any form cannot make people righteous and holy in God's eyes.

(3) recognize that you cannot devise your own way to God. You must come to God on His terms not your own. (Exodus 20:3-5) Religion is man devising his own way to God whereas the true gospel message of Biblical Christianity is God reaching down to man His way, in which He revealed His way to Himself in Christ. (Genesis 3:9, Luke 19:10)

(4) recognize that God's way demands that the sentence of death be exacted upon sinful man for his rebellion against a holy and just God (though He was sinless, Jesus, as a man, was executed in our place). The demands of a holy God for justice to be paid in blood is pictured in the Old Testament sacrificial system given to Israel through the Levitical Law. This is somewhat summarized in Hebrews 9:22. The writer of Hebrews however goes on to point out that this temporary earthly symbol of a sacrificial system was insufficient to cleanse the worshippers of God as stated in Hebrews

10:1-4. He then brings out that this sacrificial system was only a *"shadow"* of the real sacrifice that was necessary to bring us into a right relationship with God and that, of course, was the totally sufficient sacrifice of Christ. (Hebrews 10:5-10)

(5) recognize that we are to have faith in Christ alone and His atoning work for our salvation. Our faith in Christ must be exclusive of every other religious system, teaching, creed, or person, including trusting in our own selves. (Ephesians 2:8,9, Titus 3:4)

The Baptism of Jesus

In the Gospel of Matthew, chapter 3, verses 13 through 17, we read the following: *(13) "Then Jesus came from Galilee to the Jordan to be baptized by John. (14) But John tried to deter Him, saying I need to be baptized by You, and You come to me? (15) Jesus replied, 'let it be so now; it is proper for us to do this to fulfill all righteousness.' Then John consented. (16) As soon as Jesus was baptized, He went up out of the water. At that moment heaven was opened, and He saw the Spirit of God descending like a dove and alighting on Him. (17) And a voice from heaven said, 'This is my Son, whom I love; with Him I am well pleased."*

John's response to Jesus coming to him for baptism is most interesting. It appears that he is surprised that Jesus would come to him to be baptized. After all, John's baptism was a baptism of repentance from sin. His message, as can be seen in the beginning of chapter 3 in verse 2 was, *"repent, for the kingdom of heaven has come near."* The question is, why is Jesus, who was without sin, coming to be baptized by John?

I believe the answer to this has to do with the fact that Jesus, even though he was the perfect, sinless Son of God, chose to identify Himself with the lost estate of sinful man. As man is commanded by God to repent of sin and turn to God, Jesus, in turn, gives Himself to sinful man. As Jesus goes down into the water, this speaks of His death and burial on our behalf. Not only does it speak of His death, but it also speaks of the death of our old sinful self.

For a person to trust Christ to be their Savior, they need to see themselves from God's perspective as a lost sinner deserving death in need of a perfect Savior. When Jesus died on the cross and was buried, so it was, from God's perspective, God carried out His sentence of death upon us in Christ.

We also see from this that as Jesus arose out of the water, God the Father sent the Holy Spirit to Jesus in the form of a dove, at which time, God the Father pronounced that Jesus was His Son in whom He was well pleased. As Christ arose from the death that was due us, so we arise in His new life. The apostle Paul wrote about this union that we have in Christ in his letter to the Romans in 6:5-8 which says, *(5) "If we have been united with Him in His death, we will certainly also be united with Him in his resurrection. (6) For we know that our old self was crucified with Him so that the body of sin might be rendered powerless, that we should no longer be slaves to sin---(7) because anyone who has died has been freed from sin. (8) Now if we died with Christ, we believe that we will also live in Him."*

As a personal testimony to this, the apostle Paul wrote of this in his letter to the Galatians in chapter 2, verse 20, *"I have been crucified with Christ and I no longer live, but Christ lives in me. The life I live in the body, I live by faith in the Son of God, who loved me and gave Himself for me."* This verse is of course instructive to the Galatians and to us as well.

As Baptists, regarding believer's baptism, when a person is baptized by immersion, we often say, "buried with Christ in baptism, raised to walk in newness of life."

The Temptation of Christ
Matthew 4:1-5

Here we see Jesus being led of the Spirit into the desert to be tempted by Satan just prior to the beginning of His earthly ministry. This was a formative time for Him in which He obtains from the scriptures the direction He needed to carry out His earthly ministry of presenting Himself as the Son of God, Israel's Messiah, and the

Savior of mankind. From an evangelistic standpoint we will be looking at the first temptation to turn stones into bread when he was at the point of starvation.

In sharing our faith with someone, trying to ascertain their spiritual condition, we might ask the question, why do you think that God should allow you into heaven? In answer to this question people might tell you how God has met some material or physical need they may have had in their finances or healing. They may even point to a specific instance where God met these needs in an inexplicable way. In response to this, we then could share Matthew 5:45 with them which says, *"He causes the sun to rise on the evil and the good, and sends the rain on the righteous and the unrighteous."* and Psalms 145:9, which says, *"The Lord is good to all; He has compassion on all He has made."* We should go on to explain that just because God has blessed someone in a material or physical way, this is not the basis of having a right relationship with God.

Jesus's answer to Satan and His message to man, which is a quote from Deuteronomy 8:3, was, *"Man does not live by bread alone, but on every word that comes from the mouth of God."* Jesus knew that man's greatest need was spiritual, not physical, in which man's restored relationship to God through His atoning sacrifice was the thing that was of the utmost importance.

The Bronze Snake

In John's Gospel, chapter 3, we see a member of the Jewish council named Nicodemus coming to Jesus at night under the cloak of darkness. Before he can even ask a question of Jesus, Jesus immediately addresses Nicodemus's reason for coming to him and that was to ask the question, how can a person be sure they have eternal life. Jesus then tells him that for this to happen, the person needs to be born again, explaining that this is a spiritual rebirth. Jesus then refers to the wind commenting that a person can hear it, but one cannot tell where it comes from or where it is going. He then says in verse *(8), "so it is with everyone born of the Spirit."* To which Nicodemus asks in verse *(9), "How can this be?"* Jesus goes on to tell him in verse *(13), "No one has ever gone into heaven except the One who came from heaven--- The Son of Man."*

What does all this mean? It means that in the way that we recognize the fact that we do not have control over the wind, *"It blows wherever it wishes",* so too, in the same way, we need to recognize that we cannot, in and of our own selves control our being able to go to heaven. Jesus then tells Nicodemus in verse *(15), "that everyone who believes may have eternal life in Him."* (This is repeated in verse 16.) As an illustration of what it means to believe in Him, Jesus tells Nicodemus in verse *(14), "just as Moses lifted up the snake in the wilderness, so the Son of Man must be lifted up."* He, of course, was referring to his own death on a cross, drawing an analogy between his death for our sin to the time when God commanded Moses to fashion a bronze snake and put it on a pole and to lift it up for all the people to see. The reference to this incident is taken from the Old Testament book of Numbers 21:4-9. We can presume that Nicodemus, being a spiritual leader in Israel would have been familiar with this passage. Nevertheless, the setting and context of this passage is that Moses was leading a new generation of Israelites to the promise land of Canaan after wandering forty years in the desert. They, like the generation before them were prone to be rebellious. We read the following from this account, *(5) "They spoke against God and against Moses, and said, 'Why have you brought us up out of Egypt to die in the wilderness? There is no bread! There is no water! And we detest this miserable food!' (6) Then the Lord sent venomous snakes among them; (7) The people came to Moses and said, 'We sinned when we spoke against the Lord and against you. Pray that the Lord will take the snakes away from us.' So, Moses prayed for the people. (8) The Lord said to Moses, 'make a snake and put it on a pole; anyone that is bitten can look at it and live.' (9) So, Moses made a bronze snake and put it on a pole. Then when anyone was bitten by a snake and looked at the bronze snake they lived."*

How does this analogy help us to believe on Christ for our salvation? We, like they, need to:

(1) realize that we are living in rebellion against a holy and just God.

(2) call upon God for forgiveness, confessing our sin in repentance.

(3) realize that God is just in sending the penalty of death upon us for our sin and rebellion. God cannot just overlook our sin. On the other hand, God is rich in love and mercy toward us. He wants to forgive us.

(4) realize that the cure for the penalty of death comes from God alone. Remember what Jesus said in John 3:13, *"No one has ever gone into heaven except the One who came from heaven--- the Son of Man."* He alone is our cure. The Israelites were told to look to the bronze snake. We are told to look to Jesus dying upon the cross. Those who believe God and take Him at His word will live. The question is, why did God tell Moses to fashion a snake? I believe it has to do with the fact that a snake symbolizes evil and sin and God's curse upon it. We of course, see this in the account of man's fall because of Adam and Eve's sin in Genesis 3:1-7, and 14-15. Why does Jesus identify Himself with the symbol of evil and sin in John 3:14? The apostle Paul gives us the answer to this in II Corinthians

5:21 which says, *"God made Him who had no sin to be sin* (some versions, *a sin offering*) *for us, so that in Him we might become* (*"be made"* KJV) *the righteousness of God."* Even though Jesus was sinless, God the Father poured out His wrath on Him at the cross as if He were a guilty sinner. For those who look to Him as a payment for their sin, God pardons that person, imputing to that person the very righteousness of Christ.

Isaiah the prophet expressed it this way some seven hundred years before Christ in Isaiah 53:5-6, *(5) "But He was pierced for our transgressions, He was crushed for our iniquities, the punishment that brought us peace was on Him, and by His wounds we are healed. (6) We all, like sheep have gone astray, each of us has turned to our own way; and the Lord has laid on Him the iniquity of us all.*

From II Corinthians 5:21 and Isaiah 53:5-6 we see that when Jesus died on the cross, God transferred all our sin and guilt upon Christ while transferring all of Jesus's righteousness to us. In Christ, God provided this total exchange to all who repent and believe on Christ.

The Gospel of Peace
Ephesians 6:15

The gospel described in Ephesians 6:15 is described as the gospel of peace. This aspect of the gospel is speaking to the issue of the need for reconciliation to take place between a holy and just God and sinful man. For man to really see his need for God's forgiveness, he needs to see himself from God's perspective. We need to realize that our sin and sin nature is an offense to God. God is the offended party. The nature of our offense is our rebellion against His rightful rule and place as the God of His creation and of our individual lives. The essence of sin lies in our rebellion against Him. C.S. Lewis, in his book, "Mere Christianity", described sin as our being the god of our lives, denying God His rightful place as God. **(2)** We selfishly live self-centered lives instead of God centered lives. The problem is that we are the one in control. If we were to define sin in its simplest terms, it could be illustrated as the word S(I)N, recognizing that the letter "I" is at the center. God's view of man's sinful nature is described Romans 8:6-8, which says, *(6) "The mind of sinful man is death, but the mind controlled by the Spirit is life and peace;(7) the sinful mind is hostile to God. It does not submit to God's law, nor can it do so. (8) Those controlled by the sinful nature cannot please God."* Ephesians 2:1 says, *"As for you, you were dead in your transgressions and sins"* Consequently, Ephesians 2:3 tells us that *"Like the rest, we were by nature the children of wrath."* Romans 6:23 tells us *"For the wages of sin is death..."*

If we get what we deserve, we get death. This, according to Romans 6:23 is what have we earned. No amount of good works or religion or trying to be a good person on our part will overcome our sin nature, which is, as we read in Romans 8:7 is that *"the sinful mind is hostile to God."* Romans 5:12 tells us that we all inherited this nature due to the sin of the first man Adam. Therefore, the sentence of death comes to all of us because we have all sinned. This is the dilemma of man's lost estate before a holy and righteous God.

On the other hand, we see from this passage in Ephesians 2:4-5 that God loves us and is rich in His mercy towards us. II Peter 3:9 tells us that, *"…He is patient with you, not wanting anyone to perish, but everyone to come to repentance."*

The question is, how can God, who is holy and just, extend this love and forgiveness to the one who has rebelled against Him, when His very nature demands that the just penalty of death be exacted upon man for this offense? The answer to this is in His preordained plan in which He would send His Son Jesus, as a man, who was the perfect Lamb of God, to pay the penalty for our sin(s). Romans 5:8 says, *"But God demonstrates His own love for us in this: While we were still sinners, Christ died for us."* John 3:16 says, *"For God so loved the world that He gave His one and only Son, that whoever believes in Him shall not perish but have eternal life."*

Jesus, as God's Son, according to God the Father's will, voluntarily yielded up His life as a perfect payment for our offense. The death He died was done on our behalf as a substitutionary death in our place. Hebrews 2:9 tells us that, *"...He suffered death, so that by the grace of God, He might taste death for everyone."*

In this way, God could demonstrate to man the extent of His love toward man without violating His righteous demand for the penalty of death to be executed upon man. His righteous anger toward man for his rebellion against Him would be totally satisfied when He exacted the penalty of death on His Son as a man in our place.

Some seven hundred years before the coming of Christ, under the inspiration of God the Holy Spirit, the prophet Isaiah wrote about man's restoration and reconciliation with God through the sacrifice of Christ in Isaiah 53. This message was written in graphic detail to which we might pay particular attention to verses 4-6 and 10 and to the summary given in verse 12 which says, *"...He poured out His life unto death... for He bore the sin of many..."*

In addition to His dying as a sacrifice for our sin(s) in our place, King David prophesied of Christ's resurrection in Psalm 16:9-10, which says, *(9) "Therefore my heart is glad and my tongue rejoices, my body will also rest secure, (10) because you will not abandon me to the grave, nor will you let your Holy One see decay."*

In fulfillment of this prophecy, Jesus, on several occasions, told His disciples that He would be killed by the chief priests and the teachers of the law, then after three days He would rise from the dead. (Matthew 16:21,17:22-23, 26:31-32, and Mark 9:9) In answer to the Jewish leader's demand for a miraculous sign from Jesus to prove His authority to cleanse the temple, Jesus responded by saying, *"Destroy this temple, and I will raise it again in three days."* (John 2:18-19) In Matthew 12:38-40 we read, *(38) "Then some of the pharisees and teachers of the law said to Him, 'Teacher, we want to see a miraculous sign from you.' (39) He answered, 'A wicked and adulterous generation asks for a miraculous sign! But none will be given it except the sign of the prophet Jonah. (40) For as Jonah was three days and three nights in the belly of a huge fish, so the Son of Man will be three days and three nights in the heart of the earth."* In both these instances Jesus was referring to His death and His resurrection after three days. Though Jesus performed countless miracles during His earthly ministry, the miracle of His resurrection is the one miracle that validates the fact that this Jesus of Nazareth is the Son of God, the prophesied Holy One, the Savior of man. Toward the end of each of the four Gospels in the New Testament we have the recorded eyewitness accounts of Jesus's resurrection. In the book of Acts, Chapter 1, we have a continuation of those accounts along with the eyewitness account of His bodily ascension into heaven.

Not only is Jesus's resurrection a validation of the fact that He is the Son of God, but this fact is crucial to the work of this salvation He offers us according to I Corinthians

15:17, which says, *"And if Christ has not been raised, your faith is futile; you are still in your sins."* To this point we also read in Romans 4:25, *"He was delivered to death for our sins and was raised to life for our justification."*

The question then becomes, how does a person receive the benefit of this restoration and reconciliation back to God that He offers to us through the work of Christ? The answer to this is given in verse 1 of Isaiah 53, which says, *"Who has believed our message ...?"* We receive this salvation when we believe in Him, or put another way, when we put our faith in Him. Ephesians 2:8-9 tells us that, (8) *"For it is by grace you have been saved, through faith - and this not from yourselves, it is the gift of God – not by works, so that no one can boast."* What does it mean to put our faith in Him? It means that we put our faith in Him for who He is and for what He has done. Our faith in Him begins when we realize that we are a sinner, who is spiritually bankrupt and destitute, in need of the Savior. (Matthew 5:3) The question is not however, is Jesus the Savior. This is nothing more than an intellectual acceptance of historical facts! The question is, is Jesus <u>my</u> Savior?

When we recognize God for who He is, we recognize that He is faithful and true to His Word. We can fully trust Him to save us as we entrust our lives and souls to Him. We recognize that He is the Lord Jesus Christ. We must come to a place where we are willing to accept His Lordship over our lives. That means that we are willing for Him to take over the controls of our lives. When we come to Him, (as He is the One drawing us unto Himself), we come in unconditional surrender to His Lordship.

We have already covered the basic elements of what He has done for us as our Savior, except to say that we must place our faith in Him and what He has done completely. This means that we dare not trust in anything except the finished work of Christ. This would include doing anything that is associated with the usual religious activities and practices of being a church member such as being baptized, going forward during an alter call, being active in the church, having a leadership position in the church, giving a tithe to the church, reading the Bible, attending Bible study, prayer, even being involved in evangelism, and good works, etc. There is nothing wrong with these things if they are the result of our trusting Christ alone but if we trust in these or any kind of religious activity and or status instead of putting our full faith in Christ alone, then we have said to God, what Christ did on the cross was insufficient to save me. To do so is an insult to God. With regards to this, Jesus gave an illustration contrasting the old covenant law with the new covenant, in which He tells us in Matthew 9:16-17, that, *(16) "No one sews a patch of unshrunk cloth on an old garment, for the patch will pull away from the garment making the tear worse. (17) Neither do men pour new wine into old wineskins. If they do, the skins will burst, the wine will run out and the wineskins will be ruined. No, they pour new wine into new wineskins, and both are preserved."* We cannot *"patch"* up our lives with religious and sometimes Christian religious practices and think that our robe of righteousness before God is acceptable to Him. No, we need to realize that our robe of righteousness before Him is as filthy rags. (Isaiah 64:6) What we need is a whole new beautiful garment that only God Himself can provide. We need to realize that only He can give us the robe of righteousness that is acceptable to Him. Similarly, we should not expect that God will pour the Holy Spirit of the risen Christ into our old unregenerated lives.

Just before Jesus died on the cross, He said *"tetelestai,"* which means *"It is finished."* This is a marketplace or an accounting term which means, the debt that was owed has been paid in full. When Jesus ascended into heaven, the scripture in Hebrews 10:12 tells us, *"But when this priest* (Jesus) *had offered for all time one sacrifice* (Himself) *for sins, He sat down at the right hand of God."* His sacrifice for us is all sufficient. We dare not substitute anything for it or add anything to it, but rather put our total trust and faith in Him and what He has done for us. When a person puts their trust and faith in Christ in this way, God is faithful according to His word, to forgive our sins and our sinful lives justifying us before Himself in Christ. This means we stand blameless before Him because of the righteousness of Christ, which He has given to us when we believe on Him. The apostle Paul, in his letter to the Romans, in Romans

5:1-2 wrote, *(1) "Therefore since we have been justified through faith, we have peace with God through our Lord Jesus Christ, (2) through whom we have gained access by faith into this grace in which we now stand...",* and to the Colossians He wrote in Colossians 1:19-23, *(19) "For God was pleased to have all His fullness dwell in Him, (20) and through Him to reconcile to Himself all things, whether things on earth or things in heaven by making peace through His blood shed on the cross.(21) Once you were alienated from God and were enemies in your minds because of your evil behavior. (22) But now He has reconciled you by Christ's physical body through death to present you holy in His sight, without blemish and free from accusation — (23) if you continue in your faith, established and firm, not moved from the hope held out in the gospel."* When we believe on Christ, we have peace with God because He has reconciled us to Himself in Him. According to II Corinthians 5:18, *"All this is from God, who reconciled us to Himself through Christ and gave us the ministry of reconciliation."* The apostle Paul admonishes us in Ephesians 6:14 and 15 to *(14) "Stand firm... (15) ... having shod your feet with the gospel of peace;"* (NASB)

The Workers in the Vineyard

Jesus told this parable recorded in Matthew's Gospel, chapter 20, verses 1-16 saying, *(1) "For the kingdom of heaven is like a landowner who went out early in the morning to hire workers for his vineyard. (2) He agreed to pay them a denarius for the day and sent them into his vineyard."* Later he went out to hire more around nine, at noon, and then around three in the afternoon telling them, *(4) "...I will pay you whatever is right."* He later hired more workers around five in the afternoon telling them, *(7) "... you also go and work in my vineyard." (8) When evening came, the owner of the vineyard said to his foreman, 'call the workers and pay them their wages beginning with the last ones hired and going on to the first.' (9) The workers who were hired about five in the afternoon came and each received a denarius. (10) So, when those came who were hired first, they expected to receive more. But each one of them also received a denarius. (11) When they received it, they began to grumble against the landowner. (12) 'These who were hired last worked only one hour, they said, 'you have made them equal to us, who have borne the burden of the work and the heat of the day.'(13) But he answered one of them, 'I am not being unfair with you friend. Didn't you agree to work for a denarius? (14) Take your pay and go. I want to give the one who was hired last the same as I gave you. (15) Don't I have the right to do what I want with my own money? Or are you envious because I am generous? (16) So, the last will be first and the first will be last."*

We must keep in mind that a parable usually stresses one main point. First off, we see that this parable is a parable that shows something about the kingdom of heaven. As such, we see that the main thing being taught is, how do we view our relationship to God as it relates to what we think we deserve from God.

The first thing we see in this parable is the difference in how the landowner paid the early workers by agreeing to pay them one denarius with those he hired later at nine, noon and three saying, *"I will pay you whatever is right."* To those he hired at five he simply hired them without agreeing on a salary. With those he hired later in the day, he hired them based on trusting him to do the right thing. When he paid those he hired early in the morning the same amount of one denarius as he paid the other workers, they began to complain, accusing him of being unfair, asserting that they deserved to be paid more. The landowner then reminds them that they agreed to receive one denarius; therefore, he was not being unfair with them. He then told them that he had a right to do whatever he wanted with his money.

The point is that people should realize that no amount of good works is going to put God in a position in which He owes you anything. In other words, we cannot obligate God to give us what we think we have earned or deserve. This is the problem with most religious systems.

The right attitude toward God is trusting Him to do *"whatever is right"* and not expecting God to give us what we think we deserve. The apostle Paul spoke to this issue in his letter to the Romans in chapter 11, verse 35, which says, *"Who has given to God, that God should repay them?"* This is a quote from the book of Job, chapter 41, verse 11, in which it is stated this way, *"Who has a claim against me that I must pay?"* This is one of God's responses to Job at the end of the book after Job's physical trial. Job complains that he does not deserve his trial to his three accusers, while trying to justify himself by asserting his own righteousness.

We are accountable to God. He is not accountable to us. Let us appeal to God based on His graciousness toward us like the Psalmist did in Psalms 6:2 and 4, which says, *(2) "Be gracious to me, O Lord… (4) … save me because of Thy lovingkindness."* When we approach God in this way, realizing that Jesus paid the penalty for our sin, God then says to us, *"For it is by grace you have been saved, through faith – and this is not from yourselves, it is the gift of God – not by works, so that no one can boast."* (Ephesians 2:8-9)

CHAPTER 3
BIBLICAL ANSWERS TO OBJECTIONS

I'm a Pretty Good Person

Quite often a person will answer, "I'm a pretty good person" when asked the question, why do you think God should allow you into heaven?

We could then ask that person the question, what do you mean by good? More than likely, we might get a response like, well, I am not a criminal, or I have been a good wife, or husband or parent or a dutiful child or the like. They may say something like, I am a hard-working, responsible citizen. They might even list several things that are of a charitable nature which they are involved in. All in all, they consider themselves to be a pretty good person. They surmise that their goodness outweighs whatever faults they may have, and on that basis, God will accept them into heaven.

In response to this, we could share with them the account which took place between a rich young man and Jesus, that is written in all three of the synoptic Gospel records. In Matthew 19:16-26 we read, *(16) "Now a man came up to Jesus and asked, 'Teacher, what good thing must I do to get eternal life?' (17) 'Why do you ask me about what is good?', Jesus replied. There is only One who is good.* (Mark 10:18 adds, *"except God alone"*) *If you want to enter life, obey the commandments.' (18) 'Which ones?' the man replied. Jesus replied, 'Do not murder, do not commit adultery, do not steal, do not give false testimony, (19) honor your father and mother, and love your neighbor as yourself.' (20) 'All these I have kept,' the young man said. 'What do I still lack?' (21) Jesus answered, 'If you want to be perfect, go sell your possessions and give to the poor, and you will have treasure in heaven. Then come, follow Me.' (22) When the young man heard this, he went away sad, because he had great wealth. (23) Then Jesus said to His disciples, 'I tell you the truth, it is hard for a rich man to enter the kingdom of heaven. (24) Again, I tell you, it is easier for a camel to go through the eye of a needle than for a rich man to enter the kingdom of God.'(25) When the disciples heard this, they were greatly astonished, and asked, 'Who then can be saved?' (26) Jesus looked at them and said, 'with man this is impossible, but with God all things are possible."* By outward appearances to society at large, this man was a good person. (This is indicated by the reaction of the disciples to Jesus's comment, *"It is easier for a camel to go through the eye of a needle than for a rich man to enter the kingdom of God."*)

Despite this, the young man had doubts about his relationship with God, hence his question in verse 16.

In response, in typical fashion, Jesus posed a question in verse 17 which says, *"Why do you ask Me about what is good?* (then) *Jesus replied, 'There is only One who is good.* (Mark 10:18 goes on to say, '*No one is good except God alone.*')

Jesus then confined his answer written in verse 17 to, *"If you want to enter life, obey the commandments."* This was in strict response to the man's question in verse 16 of *"… what good thing must I do to get eternal life?"* The man then asked, *"which ones",* indicating that he thought that he might be accepted by God by a partial keeping of God's commandments. Jesus then cites those laws which He knew the man thought he had kept. Because he still had doubt about his acceptance from God, the man asked in verse 20 *"What do I still lack?"* Jesus then puts His finger on this man's particular sin, which, according to the keeping of the law, in letter, and in spirit, was greed.

In addition to this passage, we need to look at Galatians 5:3 and James 2:10. Galatians 5:3 says, *"Again I declare to every man who lets himself be circumcised, that he is obligated to obey the whole law."* (Within the context, circumcision is a symbol for trying to come to God based upon keeping God's moral law.) James 2:10 says, *"For whoever keeps the whole law and yet stumbles at just one point, is guilty of breaking all of it."*

The answer to the person who thinks that he or she is acceptable to God based upon their own goodness must realize that, according to these scriptures, they are obligated to obey the entire law perfectly. Galatians goes on to tell us in Galatians 3:10, *"All who rely on observing the law are under a curse, for it is written: Cursed is everyone who does not continue to do everything written in the Book of the Law."* (a quote from Deuteronomy 27:26) Based upon God's moral law, none of us are good, and as such, we are all under God's curse.

But thanks be to God, our story does not end there. Galatians 3:13 goes on to tell us, *"Christ redeemed us from the curse of the law by becoming a curse for us, for it is written: Cursed is everyone who is hung on a tree."* (a quote from Deuteronomy 21:23) Like a criminal sentenced to death under the Old Testament Law, Christ was hung on a tree (crucified), taking God's curse that was due us upon Himself. Galatians 3:14 then tells us that, *"He redeemed us that in order that the blessing given to Abraham might come to the Gentiles through Christ Jesus, so that by faith we might receive the promise of the Spirit."*

In answer to the disciple's question, *"Who then can be saved,"* in our account of the rich young man and Jesus in Matthew 19:25, Jesus gives them and us the answer in Matthew 19:26, which says, *"...with man this is impossible, but with God all things are possible."* In his letter to Titus in Titus 3:4, the apostle Paul goes on to tell us, *"But when the kindness and love of God our Savior appeared, He saved us, not because of righteous things we have done, but because of His mercy."*

I owed a debt I could not pay; He paid a debt He did not owe.

I Don't Want to Leave My Friends

At the core of this issue, it may be that the person does not want to leave a sinful lifestyle that he or she has in common with their circle of friends. This of course, would mean giving up whatever sinful pleasures they think they are getting. To this we could share that Romans 6:19-23 tells us that apart from Christ we are slaves to sin which results in death. But when we become a slave to God, we derive the benefit of sanctification which results in eternal life. This is summarized in Romans 6:23, which says, *"For the wages of sin is death, but the free gift of God is eternal life in Christ Jesus our Lord.* (NASB) Psalms 1:1,6 puts it this way, *(1) "How blessed is the man who does not walk in the counsel of the wicked, Nor stand in the path of sinners, nor sit in the seat of scoffers! (6) For the Lord knows the way of the righteous, But the of the way of wicked will perish."* (NASB)

Or it could be that they genuinely just want to keep their friendship or affection, fearing that if they accept Christ, their friend will leave them. Jesus spoke to this issue in Matthew 10:34-39. Here He tells us that as His disciple, our loyalty is preeminently to Him, even over our own family. This certainly would hold true for being loyal to Him over our friends. Proverbs 12:26 tells us that, *"The righteous choose their friends carefully, but the way of the wicked lead them astray."*

This of course, does not mean that we, as Christians, are to adopt a monk like lifestyle separating ourselves from unbelievers. These are the very people who need to hear the message of salvation that will come from our lips. With regards to this, we read the following from Matthew 9:9-13, *(9) "As Jesus went on from there, He saw a man named Matthew sitting at the tax collector's booth. 'Follow me' He told him, and Matthew got up and followed Him. (10) While Jesus was having dinner at Matthew's house, many tax collectors and sinners came and ate with Him and His disciples. (11) When the pharisees saw this, they asked His disciples, 'Why does your teacher eat with tax collectors and sinners?' On hearing this, Jesus said, 'It is not the healthy who need a doctor, but the sick. (13) But go and learn what this means: I desire mercy, not sacrifice. For I have not come to call the righteous, but sinners."*

Jesus then tells His disciples and us in John 20:21, *"... As the Father has sent Me, I am sending you."*

With these passages in mind, how are we to interact with the lost after we have received Christ? We find some direction regarding this from the book of Jude:23, which says, *"save others by snatching them from the fire; to others, show mercy, mixed with fear-hating even the clothing stained by corrupted flesh."*

We are to influence the lost, trying to win them over to Christ, being careful not to allow them and their sinful lifestyles to draw us into sin. But, when it comes to our more intimate relationships such as marriage, business partners, and close friends, we are told in II Corinthians 6:14, *"Do not be yoked together with unbelievers. For what do righteousness and wickedness have in common? Or what fellowship can light have with darkness?"*

I Don't Need a Savior

How do we respond to a person that tells you, I don't need a Savior? Ask the question, may I share with you what the Bible says about our need of a Savior? If they say yes, then lovingly share the gospel with them. As part of that presentation, our objective should be to show the person their lives from God's perspective. This, of course, means that we share with them about our lost estate because of our rebellion against a Holy God. We might ask the person if they are familiar with the Bible verse John 3:16. As a reminder, we should quote this verse, commenting on God's love for us by giving us His Son as a sacrifice for our sins. Then, we need to elaborate on the fact that this same passage also speaks to the fact that we are presently under condemnation without Jesus as our Savior. Jesus Himself said in John 3:18, *"Whoever believes in Him* (referring to Himself) *is not condemned, but whoever does not believe in Him stands condemned already because he has not believed the name of God's one and only Son."* Then at the end of that chapter we have John the Baptist's testimony about Jesus in which he concludes, by saying in John 3:36, *"Whoever believes in the Son has eternal life, but whoever rejects the Son will not see life, for God's wrath remains on him."* The apostle Paul summarizes our lost condition in his letter to the Romans in Romans 3:23 and 6:23, which says, *(3:23) "For all have sinned and fall short of the glory of God," and (6:23) "For the wages of sin is death..."*

The following illustration could be used to demonstrate man's dilemma and God's predetermined solution to it.

You are arrested and charged with the high crime of rebellion against the king. The penalty for this crime, if convicted, is death. At your court hearing, you appear before the king who is also the judge of the land. The evidence against you is compelling and you are found guilty. In this case, the judge is just. He informs you that you are guilty and that your sentence is death. But he is also rich in mercy and wants to forgive you, but he informs you that your crime demands the penalty of death. In this case your defense attorney is the king's only son. The king and the son have arranged a plea bargain in which the son agrees to pay your penalty of death for you. The son then informs you that even though he will undergo being put to death on your behalf, he has complete faith in his father, that the father will bring him back to life. Knowing all this, the condition of your forgiveness is that you are truly sorry for your crime and that you accept the son's payment on your behalf, being willing to allow the son to be your master for the rest of your life.

Put another way, God is giving guilty sinners a chance to settle our case with Him out of court. He offers us a plea bargain in which we throw ourselves at the mercy of the court, accepting His gracious offer of forgiveness at His expense. When we do this, He writes our names in the book of life. If we do not accept His offer, we will have to appear before His great white throne of judgement and condemnation. (Revelation 20:11-15)

For Those Who Say, Not Now

Jesus speaking in John 6:44 tells us that, *"No one can come to Me unless the Father who sent Me draws him, and I will raise him up at the last day."* He also said in Luke 19:10, *"For the Son of Man came to seek and save what was lost."* When Adam and Eve sinned against God, they ran and hid themselves from Him in guilty fear. It was God who was the One who called out to them, *"Where are you?"* (Genesis 3:9) God is the One who sought an audience with them. Psalms 32:6 tells us, *"Therefore let everyone who is Godly pray to You while You may be found; surely when the mighty rivers rise, they will not reach Him."* Isaiah 49:8 says, *"This is what the Lord says: In the time of My favor, I will answer you, and in the day of salvation I will help you."* (Isaiah 49:8 was quoted by the apostle Paul in II Corinthians 6:2.) Isaiah 55:6 says,

"Seek the Lord while He may be found; call on Him while He is near." From these verses we see that it is God who is the One who determines what is the acceptable time in which a person can respond to Him. It is *"in the time of His favor"*, that He offers His salvation. The lost dare not presume upon God's graciousness by telling Him that they will come to Him when they decide later. Proverbs 27:1 says, *"Do not boast about tomorrow, for you do not know what a day may bring forth."* Matthew 24:44 tells us, *"So, you also must be ready, because the Son of Man will come at an hour when you do not expect Him."*

The fact of the matter is that when a person rejects God's gracious offer of salvation *"in the day of His favor,"* their heart may be hardened against God to the point where they never accept His offer. The person needs to realize that they are totally at God's mercy. Therefore, Hebrews 3:7 tells us, *"So, as the Holy Spirit says: 'Today, if you hear His voice, do not harden your hearts as you did in the rebellion…"* Hebrews 3:12-13 says, *(12) "See to it brothers that none of you has a sinful unbelieving heart that turns away from the living God. But encourage one another daily, as long as it is called Today, so that none of you may be hardened by sin's deceitfulness."* Consequently, the writer of Hebrews says in Hebrews 3:15, and again in Hebrews 4:7, *"Today, if you hear His voice, do not harden your hearts…"* Then in Hebrews 2:1-3a, the writer tells us that, *(1) "We must pay more careful attention, therefore, to what we have heard, so that we do not drift away. (2) For if the message spoken by angels was binding, and every violation and disobedience received its just punishment, (3) how shall we escape if we ignore (neglect* NASB*) such a great salvation?"*

And so, we may want to lovingly encourage a person to not put off receiving Christ as Lord and Savior, maybe sharing some of these verses with them. At the same time, we should remind them that, *"...He is patient with you, not wanting anyone to perish, but everyone to come to repentance."* (II Peter 3:9b) I believe that when we share Christ in this way, we will have done so in accordance with Colossians 4:6, which says, *"Let your conversation be always full of grace, seasoned with salt, so that you may know how to answer everyone."*

Remember, *"The fear of the Lord is the beginning of wisdom..."* (Proverbs 1:7)

CHAPTER 4

Christian Apologetics

------- ◆◆◆◆◆ -------

Science and the Bible

Sometimes people will say something like, "I believe in science, not the Bible". The implication of this statement is that the two are mutually exclusive.

Websters Secondary School Dictionary (copyright 1932) defines science as:

(1) Knowledge, as of principles or facts
(2) Accumulated and accepted knowledge systematized and formulated with reference to the discovery of general truths or the operation of general laws

Today's definition of science however is not the same as it was in the past. L. Pearce Williams wrote the following in his article entitled, "History of Science", "On the simplest level, science is knowledge of the world of nature ..." Then later in the article he wrote: "If the history of science is to make any sense whatsoever, it is necessary to deal with the past on its own terms, and the fact is that for most of the history of science, natural philosophers appealed to causes that would be summarily rejected by modern scientists. Spiritual and divine forces were accepted as both real and necessary until the end of the 18th century and, in areas such as biology, deep into the 19th century as well." **(3)**

Today's definition of science, for the most part by the scientific community at large, only recognizes man's discovery of the natural world through observation and experimentation. **(4)** This, of course, is a very humanistic view of science. This view discounts the fact that knowledge of the natural world can also be obtained and or be aided by the divine revelation of God through His written Word.

Contrary to this humanistic view of science, the scriptures tell us that, *"The secret things belong to the Lord our God, but the things revealed belong to us and our children forever, that we may follow all the words of this law,"* (Deuteronomy 29:29) and that, *"It is the glory of God to conceal a matter; to search out a matter is the glory of kings,* (Proverbs 25:2) and that, *"He reveals deep and hidden things; He knows what lies in darkness, and light dwells with Him."* (Daniel 2:22)

To the children of Israel, God tells them in Amos 3:7 that, *"Surely the Lord does nothing unless He reveals His secret counsel to His servants the prophets."*

There are several scriptures in the Old Testament in which God tells us much about the natural world. These were written hundreds and sometimes thousands of years before man discovered them. This is not to suggest of course, that the Bible is a science book but rather to show that these scriptures taken together with all the fulfilled prophecies in the Bible demonstrate that the Bible is divinely inspired by God. As such, the Bible tells us in Genesis 1:1, *"In the beginning God created the heavens and the earth",* and in Psalms 100:3, *"Know that the Lord Himself is God; It is He who has made us, not we ourselves..."* (NASB)

In response to their creation, Psalms 19:1 tells us that, *"The heavens declare the glory of God; the skies proclaim the work of His hands."*

Using today's scientific terms, we could say that Psalms 19:1 says "(The natural world) *declares the glory of God;* (The natural world) *proclaims the work of His hands."*

The question is not, do we believe in science, or do we believe in religion or the Bible, but rather, the question is, are we willing to accept what the natural world is plainly telling us.

Romans 1:20 says, *"For since the creation of the world His invisible attributes, His eternal power and divine nature, have been clearly seen, being understood through what has been made, so that they are without excuse."* (NASB) Given the fact that it is most logical to believe that something cannot come from nothing, it then follows that even the existence of science itself is not logically possible without a Creator who created everything.

We then might share with that person a scripture taken from Hebrews 11:6, which says, *"And without faith it is impossible to please God, because anyone who comes to Him must believe that He exists and that He rewards those who earnestly seek Him."* Depending on the amount of time, the circumstances and how receptive the person is, we then could either share the gospel with them or leave the conversation open ended, offering to talk with them further about what it means to come to God on God's terms.

Prophecy Fulfilled

One of the most compelling arguments for Jesus of Nazareth being the Christ (Messiah), thus the Son of God, our Savior, is the collective record of evidence contained in the Old and the New Testaments and the Dead Sea Scrolls. These show us that Jesus fulfilled numerous Old Testament prophecies, which foretold His first coming.

Given the availability of information which refer to and make commentary about these prophecies, I will defer giving my commentary about these prophecies to those voluminous resources.

I say that, except to say that it has been known since the time of Christ that there are those critics who claim that the New Testament writers and early Christians took liberties with the Old Testament scriptures by taking them out of their historical context. These critics further accuse those Christians of reinterpreting these scriptures to make it appear that Jesus fulfilled these prophesies. Addressing this point, my comment is, yes, we need to interpret scripture within its context, but we should also recognize from the volume of evidence, that these prophetic scriptures should also be interpreted from the context of the Bible as a whole. In addition to these prophecies, the Old Testament is interwoven throughout with all kinds of types and *"shadows",* all of which point us to Christ. (Hebrews 8:1-5) When the Old and New testaments are taken together, we see the overriding theme of God bringing about His redemption and salvation to fallen mankind, for those who put their faith in Christ and His finished work for them.

Then, to end this discussion on an authoritative note, we need to remember what Jesus Himself said about this subject. On the road to Emmaus, with two of His followers after His resurrection, Luke recorded His words in Luke 24:25-27, which says, *(25) "He said to them, 'How foolish you are, and how slow to believe <u>all that the prophets have spoken!</u> (26) Did not the Messiah have to suffer these things and then enter His glory?' (27) And beginning with <u>Moses and all the Prophets,</u> He explained what was said <u>in all the Scriptures</u> concerning Himself."* (See also Matthew 5:17 and Luke 4:14-21.) In addition to this, we have the apostle Paul, by the inspiration of the Holy Spirit, in his summary of the gospel, in I Corinthians 15:3-4 saying, *(3) "For what I received I passed on to you as* *of first importance: that Christ died for our sins <u>according to the Scriptures</u>, (4) that He was buried, that He was raised on the third day <u>according to the Scriptures</u>."*

Annotated Bibliography

(1) This axiom is first thought to have been written by the Reverend Professor John "Rabbi" Duncan (1796-1870) and Watchman Nee in his book "Normal Christian Faith". This trilemma has since been attributed to C.S. Lewis in his book "Mere Christianity" and has in most recent years most notably been promoted by Josh McDowell and Sean McDowell PhD in their book "Evidence That Demands a Verdict", page 198. (© 2017 Josh McDowell Ministry)

(2) "Mere Christianity", page 49 Copyright ©, 1952, C.S. Lewis Pte. Ltd., Copyright renewed © 1980 C.S. Lewis Pte. Ltd. According to the internet website posted by "Onesimus" entitled "C.S. Lewis: The Roots of His Famous Quotes in the Works of George MacDonald", the article states that "George MacDonald's influence on C.S. Lewis's thought, faith, and writings was extensive enough that we might call it all-pervasive." This article goes on to say that "...Lewis himself might not always have known when he was 'borrowing' from his master (since at times he may have done so unconsciously.)"

(wwwworksofmacdonald.com/far) Among Lewis's records we have today those quotes entitled, "George MacDonald An Anthology with Preface, Edited by C.S. Lewis." (libru/LEWIS/mcdonalds_antology.txt) Under Quote (350) entitled "The Root of All Rebellion", in Chapter 15 of the book "What's Mine's Mine", MacDonald wrote, "It is because we are not near to Thee to partake of Thy liberty that we want a liberty of our own different from Thine." It appears that Lewis's description of man's rebellious state against God is a paraphrase of MacDonald's (1824-1905) earlier writing.

(3) Article by L. Pearce Williams entitled "History of Science" posted on the internet under "History of Science Definition, Natural Philosophy…Britannica" © 2021 Encyclopedia Britannica, Inc.

(4) "Scientific Method" on "Wikipedia" (https://en.wikipedia.org/wiki/Scientific_method) last edited on 16 April 2021, at 15:47 (UTC)

Made in United States
North Haven, CT
09 April 2025